In the Middle of the Night

by Amanda Graham

Secret Agent One snuck out in the middle of the night. He took a box by foot.

Secret Agent Two snuck out in the middle of the night. He took a box by horse.

Secret Agent Three snuck out in the middle of the night. He took a box by boat.

Secret Agent Four snuck out in the middle of the night. He took a box by bike.

Secret Agent Five snuck out in the middle of the night.

He took a box by train.

Secret Agent Six snuck out in the middle of the night. He took a box by car.

Secret Agent Seven snuck out in the middle of the night. He took a box by plane.

Secret Agent Eight snuck out in the middle of the night.

He took a box by submarine.

Secret Agents One, Two, Three, Four, Five, Six, Seven, and Eight …

all met at Secret Agent Nine's house.
They gave their boxes to …

Secret Agent Ten.

Surprise!

In the Middle of the Night
Small Book: ISBN 0-7406-0530-5
Small Book: ETA 252011

Big Book: ISBN 0-7406-0535-6
Big Book: ETA 252018P

Published by ETA/Cuisenaire® under license from Era Publications.
www.etacuisenaire.com

Text © 1988 by Amanda Graham
Illustration © 1988 by Amanda Graham
This edition published 2003

Printed in China. All rights reserved.

03 04 05 06 07 08 09 10 11 12   10 9 8 7 6 5 4 3 2